The Struggle of Going Nowhere

Previous books by Nanne Nyander
Silence. Angels and Poems (2018)
Out of the Labyrinth. Poems (2022)

Title: The Struggle of Going Nowhere. Poems
© Nanne Nyander 2022.
www.nannenyander.se
Published by: BoD – Books on Demand, Stockholm, Sweden
Printed by: BoD – Books on Demand, Norderstedt, Germany
Cover, book design and drawing by Nanne Nyander.
ISBN: 978-91-8057-305-4

You are Nowhere!

You are Now Here!

Love poems for the infinite.

1.

Love enters my eyes and pours out of my skin,
it lands on the ground and flows down to the river,
it unites with the ocean,
evaporates,
and becomes one with the sky,
turns into rain,
the rain is falling on my head,
it's running down my face,
entering my skin,
overflowing in my eyes,
love is pouring out of my eyes as tears,
love is falling on the ground,
my tears are entering the flowers on the ground.
Love is penetrating the fragrance of the flowers.
I pick a flower, smell it, and love enters my nose.
I breathe out,
and love becomes the air we breathe,
becomes the infinite,
love is the infinite,
I am one with everything,
I am one,
I am the infinite,
I am Love.

2.

Sounds of songs from an ancient time,
lost in my head.
Where is there, and where is here?
When is then, and when is now?
It's all a mix in this symphony of existence.
It's time to move on.
Privileged creature, beautiful me.
Savage pain, take me nowhere.

3.

It's the dream of you and me that keeps me stuck here,
give up the dream,
give up you,
give up me,
and left is nothing.
But what a beautiful nothing it is.

4.

The mist in my head is clearing up.
"Get out of the Labyrinth of your mind."
When will I finally see the truth?
Is life living me this way,
or am I living life this way?
Away from the truth of reality,
the truth of life.
I live to find out how to die,
die to find out how to live.
Life is a wonder.
I am a wonder.
"Take my hand,
and I will show you the way to be,
to be the truth."
I am, is the truth.
I am the truth.
I am.

5.

What do you see, my friend,
behind your perception of this reality?
What can you hear when everything is silent?
Here is where your true self is lingering,
here and everywhere else.

6.

Profoundly clear, is the silence you speak.
The silence is the way of the infinite to speak to me.
Can't you see it?
Can't you hear it?
Words, words, words, misunderstood words,
different meanings, same words.
Silence speaks louder and clearer
than you can ever communicate.
Silence is not a lack of words,
silence is before words,
behind them,
behind everything,
without silence,
nothing is.

7.

My wings can't take me any further.
It's time to land. It's time to stop moving.
Everything is going round in circles in my head,
I can't endure anymore.
Spread your wings over mine and let us melt into one.
Your strength will ignite mine, and I will fly yet again.
I want to fly over the moon out of joy for the one I am.

8.

Solitude is my name.
Alone I walk through life.
Nobody sees me. I can't even see me.
I'm lost in the tumultuous world
that I have created for myself.
I can't get out.
Alone I walk in this dark world.
"Let go!" I can hear you scream, or is it I?
Surrender,
give up this dark world, I tell myself, but how?
"It's a shift, shift, shift…"
I just want to scream out loud, WHAT?
I'm in pain.
"WHO is in pain?
Focus!"
Was this how I thought it would be?
Wake me up! Can't you see I'm in pain?
No, you can't, because there's nobody there.
There's Nothing here.
Solemnly I walk, I walk with my head high.
I know what I want,
even though it might cost me my sanity,
my life.
Solitude is my name,
I walk alone.

I walk alone from the darkness out into the light,
I am the light.
I am the light looking at the darkness
within and without.
Without the darkness, I am light.
With the darkness, I am light.
I am light.

9.

Resist me if you can,
hold on to yourself as if your life depended on it,
you and I will not reach victory together,
you and I will not walk together hand in hand
to the final goal and live happily ever after.
YOU have to vanish from my sight,
for me to live fully as the one that I am.
Or is it me who has to vanish?

10.

Sea of thoughts,
sea of emotions,
ocean of self.
Don't drown yourself in the sea of oblivion.
Stay with me,
stay silent,
I'm the river of life.

11.

Emptiness, silence,
I am.
I'm out of reach of the movement of the mind.
O this trickery mind.
I salvage the silence within me before it gets gulped up
by the noisy mind, the destroying force within me.
The force that does everything in its power
to distract me from what I am,
from my true identity.
I just need to stay here,
I just need to be.
I don't want to go to war with my thoughts.
They are slippery, and demanding of my attention,
like an enemy within.
An enemy that I hardly notice until it's too late.
Sleep no more,
it's time to be vigilant.
It's time to wake up.

12.

Can you look inside me,
can you see who I am,
or do you only see this shell of interpretations,
which you create in your head?
Look at me,
see me for what I am.
I'm not what you see,
I'm not what I have done,
I'm not this construction of flesh and bones,
that one day will decay and vanish.
I'm not this mind,
I'm not your interpretation of what I say, do, or write.
The best way to know me is to never have known me,
meet me with closed eyes and listen to my silence,
then you might know me.
Meet me beyond the veil of illusion.
Meet me where you and I are one.
Here you can truly know me,
as I know you.
Beyond the illusion of this made-up reality.

13.

A lullaby to myself.
My mind has been singing a lullaby to me
since I was born.
It just kept on singing without me noticing
that I was listening.
It's so familiar,
and still not.
It's familiar and yet very alien.
The feeling of losing my mind comes over me.
I'm afraid.
I'm sinking further and further into oblivion.
I can't see clearly anymore.
I feel a gentle pull,
there is something that is not letting me go,
not letting me slip further into the darkness
of the mind.
Not letting me leave this life without realising who I am.
Without realising I.
Not letting me move on to another lifetime of sorrow.
The fog is parting,
just enough for me to see the light,
the light of nothingness,
the empty space that illuminates everything,
everywhere and nowhere.
It's Nothing,
I'm only I.
I AM Nothing.

14.

Empty world, empty words.
Everyone is talking, but no one says anything.

15.

Alone am I,
alone with the whole universe.
I'm the one that will be here in the end,
when I realise the truth of what I am.
No one can walk with me. You can show me the way,
but I have to take the final step to nowhere,
where nothing meets me with open arms.
Where I can finally rest.

16.

Full moon.
The full moon is reflecting in my eyes,
shining on my face.
The moon is silent.
The silence is loud.
The moon is reflecting in my eyes.
I'm the moon which ingeniously reflects
my own beautiful silent perfection
into my own eyes.

17.

Everything is changing,
everything is in flux,
nothing is constant,
everything is pulsating.
The blood is pulsating in your veins,
the wind is breathing, pulsating,
can you feel it?
The day and the night are breathing in and out,
pulsating in the veins of the universe.
The flowers breathe in and out,
following the same rhythm.
You and I are just a breath of the totality.
Can you feel everything breathing, pulsating,
everything pulsating in perfect harmony?

18.

A love song to the ones left behind.
I will not turn around,
I will walk straight ahead with my head held up high.
No matter what you say,
no matter what you think,
I know where I'm going.
I will walk like a proud lioness,
with all the confidence worthy of the one
who dares to move ahead
despite feeling paralysed inside,
despite feeling ready to explode with all the feelings
that don't belong to me.
I'm here,
I'm out of reach,
I'm empty inside,
yet bombarded with everyone's feelings,
pulling me in all directions.
But I'm walking alone,
I'm walking straight ahead,
I'm walking tall,
with my head held high.

19.

The body makes me feel solid and stuck,
makes me feel like a bird in a cage.
Feelings are pulling me down, up, here and there,
pretending to be me.
What's going on?
Thoughts connect it all like an invisible web,
intertwined with everything and nothing.
I feel like a fly in the web of the mind,
the spider, smiling, feeling clever,
rearranging everything in the web to its benefit.
I can see a distant memory over there,
being manipulated
into something I didn't recall a minute ago.
A feeling hits me without a connecting thought,
a thought gets stuck on me, and I can't get it off.
I feel like screaming.
Is this a dream,
a never-ending nightmare?
I'm lost.
I'm not this!
Wake up!

20.

Love is not to be understood,
love is.

21.

My Beloved, let me stay with you, always.
Don't let me wander off into the forest and lose myself,
lose myself in the entanglement of thoughts.
My Beloved, I'm only here for you.
You are the reason I still breathe.
You are the reason I'm still here.
If it wasn't for you, I would have left long ago.
My determination to find you
is my reason to keep going.
My Beloved, you're like a ghost.
Trying to catch up with you is ludicrous.
I know I have to stop, and let you find me,
stop searching, stop trying,
just stop.
But will you be there to catch me if I let go,
if I stop grabbing on to illusions?
Will you be there?
My Beloved, I'm ready!
I stop, I let go, I open my eyes.
I'm the ghost, and you are real.
I am real. I'm not a ghost.
I am here, and so are you.
I AM My Beloved!
I AM.

22.

I never thought we would be together again,
you and I.
I thought I'd lost you forever.
In my dream, we were apart.
In my dream, I lost you.
Then I woke up, and saw the truth,
the truth without my dream.
Without my dream, we are together, always.
Without my dream, you and I are one.

23.

Let the rain wash away all your troubles,
because there are no troubles.
Troubles are like distant thunder.
You don't need to fear the thunder.
After the rain, the sky will be clear.
No need to dwell on the far gone thunder,
stay here and enjoy the clear sky,
stay here even when the next storm comes.

24.

The source of everything. That is you.
Why crawl around on the ground when you can fly?
Spread your wings and wake up to what you are.
Why don't you take a step back
and see this illusion for what it is,
your creation, not you.
You have got so wrapped up in the story
that you have forgotten
that you're the author of this intriguing play.
It's time to wake up!

25.

The wind caresses my naked body,
cold, fresh, purifying wind.
Sweep away all my thoughts,
expose the reality behind everything.
Leave nothing behind,
leave nothing,
leave everything,
empty me of myself.

26.

Have you ever seen the sound of silence?
Have you ever heard the sound of the clear sky?
Have you ever felt the absence
of people in a crowded room?

27.

Watch me move through space
like an angel on a mission.
The dance is in the body,
it won't stop until I find my true self.
I move without moving. I speak in silence.
I have a mission,
I'm on my way to finding myself.
With determination in my steps,
I move out of reach from the mind.
I leave it all behind for now.
I move without moving,
watching my mind go berserk,
What to do, do, do?

28.

You are lost no more when you decide to walk with me
hand in hand in the garden of Eden.
What is it like to wait for the perfect day
that will never come?
Wait no more. Come, walk with me,
hold my hand,
we're going nowhere,
and that's where you will find yourself.

29.

How can I continue the search for myself,
when I no longer believe I exist?
Watch me evaporate into space.
My ego no longer haunts me,
thoughts no longer have a gravitational pull.
More air, more space, less cloudy.
I'm here, I'm now,
I can hear you,
loud as silent music in my ears.

30.

How is it that we can talk
but not be there to receive the message?
All talk is to oneself, but no one is listening.

31.

Hope follows me wherever I go,
but sometimes I can't see it.
Is it hiding?
Or am I moving too fast?

32.

Earth in my eyes, water in my ears,
wind in my hair and fire in my heart.
Let the fire consume everything that isn't true.
Let the water give life to everything that is.
Let the wind blow away my thoughts.
Earth is vanishing from my eyes,
I can see clearly now.
It's all an illusion, nothing is real.

33.

Eyes open, I walk into the dark.
Eyes shut, I walk into the light.
This eternal darkness.
Heart closed,
I walk into the dark.
Heart open, I walk into the light.
This eternal light.

34.

Shake me till I wake up.
No more sleepwalking.
Beauty is staring me in the face,
but I can't see it.
Darkness is embracing me,
suffocating me.
Let me wake up to the sound of my own heartbeat,
beating with excitement,
excitement to finally be one with the universe,
one with you, one with I.

35.

Sweet music in my ears,
constant interruptions by the mind.
Everything goes silent,
but if you're with me, you can still hear my music.

36.

The autumn leaves,
leave me breathless.
I'm falling,
uncontrollable,
there's no bottom,
there is just empty space.
Moving,
moving through space with no mind,
I don't mind.
The autumn leaves are falling.
Catch me.
There's just emptiness,
no words, no thoughts,
no reality in the mind of the doer.
Stay, empty, space, let me fall,
keep falling, empty, silence.
Exhale, exhaustion,
no more holding on,
emptiness, stay.
No thoughts can catch me here.
I'm empty, empty, empty.
I'm the autumn leaves lost in space waiting to be found.
Not waiting anymore.
I'm not a leaf,
I'm the space in which it is all happening,
without anything happening.
I am, I am.

37.

Was I the one that started all this,
or am I a memory of the lost past
in an illusionary world?

38.

I walk through the forest of thought
in the pouring rain,
purifying water, the rain is my saviour.
It washes away everything I'm not,
leaving me totally naked.
A new beginning is upon us.
Me, myself, and I,
left is only I.
The forest is no longer a threat.
The forest is only a forest,
and I, is only I.

39.

Look into my eyes and see who I am.
I am.
Can you truly see me?

40.

I'm the warrior. I'm the peacekeeper,
I'm the one that pretends that I'm lost.
I'm the seeker who thinks she has lost
the only thing she can't ever lose.
I'm the finder of truth,
the truth that was always here.
I'm going nowhere.
I'm here.

41.

No action, no thought, just be.

42.

Was I here before I died?
Look at me now. What do you see?
Can you see me, or can you see Me?
Where are you on this road to nowhere,
no one can tell.
Listen!
I still hold your hand, or are you holding mine?
Or is there any distinction between the two?
Was I really here before,
or was it just a dream?

43.

Rest with me, open your heart, my friend,
the silence can be found where you don't look,
same place, different looking,
restless footsteps on the wet grass,
moving deeper into the centre of the labyrinth.
Turn around,
move out of the labyrinth of the mind
and find solid ground,
find the place of total silence.

44.

Let the fire inside you burn everything away,
till you're free of you,
free of all resistance,
free of everything,
free even of the urge to be free.

45.

I'm a jigsaw puzzle with plenty of missing pieces.
But it doesn't matter anymore.
The jigsaw puzzle is still an illusion.
All pieces, no pieces, or half of them missing,
what does it matter when it's all an illusion.
It might help to find all the right pieces,
but then what?
I still have to wake up.
It's all a dream,
masterly put together.

46.

I am short of time,
the end is near,
fear nothing.
This will be the culmination of my existence.
Stay as life itself,
no mind, no illusion.
Air under my wings
turns into the most magnificent sound,
lifting me from the muddy ground,
into the silent emptiness.
You're trying to catch up,
but I'm out of reach for you,
out of reach for the self.
I can see it in your eyes,
I'm dying.

47.

I'm solitude,
walking through the forest, looking for you.
Where are you?
What are you?
I'm fear, walking in your footsteps.
Can you feel me? Do you fear me?
I'm beauty walking beside you.
Can you see me?
I'm love walking in front of you,
leading you through the forest.
You can walk in my footsteps
till you've found your way out.
Leave fear to the mind.
Leave the self.
Find your way to beauty and stay with love.
You're one with love.
You're one with everything.
You ARE love.

48.

I speak a language that nobody understands.
The world is a show that I don't belong to.

49.

Illusions, illusions, illusions.
Where will it take me?
Wake up now!
I need to wake up, I need to ignore thoughts.
Everything is moving in slow motion.
I can't think straight.
Why does it feel important to think straight,
to be able to ignore thoughts?
It does not make any sense at all.
Not thinking straight or thinking very clearly indeed,
what's the difference from the perspective of the I?
None, none whatsoever.
I don't have to wait till I can be more focused,
think more clearly till I stop focusing on my mind.
It's just another trick of the ego-mind.
Everything is here now,
how can it be more or less the reality of what I am,
the truth, when I am all there is?
Be aware of non-focus,
be aware of being focused.
Be aware of the one being focused, or not focused.
Be aware of what is happening at this moment.
Be aware, be aware.
Be awake.

50.

There is no trying, there is only doing,
there is no doing, there is only being.

51.

Can I be with you when I'm gone?
I'm dissolving into nothing.
No me, no self, no ego.
Only transparent, beautiful nothing.

52.

Angelic voices in my head,
tell me I'm already it,
I'm already there.
Where to go if I'm already here?
What to do if this is it?
"Realise, realise it is so."
Nothing binds me, it's all an illusion.
The angels tell me so.

53.

Soul on its journey,
excited, happy, free.
Free to feel like it's failed.
Free to feel like it's a success.
Free to feel hurt,
free to love.

54.

We are love poems for the universe,
make a good one, make it count.
Don't leave without signing it with your true name.

55.

Will I make it through?
This body I call me, it's not me, says the mind,
which is not me either.
I can feel, I feel so intense,
these feelings must be me, says the mind,
what does the mind know, it's not me.
I remember my life, these memories have to be me,
says the mind.
What does the mind know, it's not me,
and how do I know that the mind
hasn't just made it all up,
or distorted it to its advantage.
What are memories but images and words in the mind,
which is not me.
The ego is just a concoction of feelings,
beliefs and memories,
constructed by a confusing mind.
It's not me.
How could those things be me,
I'm so much bigger than that.
I'm nothing.

56.

What about life? What about me?

57.

Look inside my mind, help me,
my true love is hiding way beyond mind,
and I am trapped.
My true love awaits me,
I want to wait no more.
My true love is patient,
I'm not.
For my true love, there is no time.
For me, every day on this treadmill is too long.
Help me!
I shout,
I scream,
I cry,
I weep.
My true love is just watching.
I yell, "Don't you care?"
I stop, feel, sense, realise,
I am the one watching.
My true love is me.

58.

Everything is connected,
my heart connects with my blood,
connects with my skin,
with the things I touch,
with the space,
with the universe,
with the infinite.
My lungs connect with the air I breathe,
connect with all the plants and trees,
connect with you,
you and I are the same,
I am you,
I am everything,
and still, I am nothing.

59.

The moment is here and now,
and now, and NOW!

60.

Outside the mind, you're no longer trapped.
Don't let the mind trap you again.
I will not abandon you!
I will stay with you till you find the way,
the way back home.
My love for you is unconditional.

61.

Here, now, feel,
be aware of who's here when no one is watching.
Who are you?
No identity left.
Random thoughts floating around in space.
Is this it?

62.

I'm left to pick up the pieces.
I feel your emotions as if they were mine,
I feel your pain as if it was my pain.
Can you feel me, my dear one?
I can't go on. I need to stop.
I need to wake up.

63.

Silence within,
there is nothing that disturbs.
Empty space between every thought,
like a comforting void of nothingness,
surrounds me with the silence that penetrates
every sound,
every bit of noise that's trying to take over this silent,
empty space.

64.

Feelings of confusion are surrounding me,
I sink under the water and disappear into oblivion.
Under the water, I can see clearly,
I can be without pretending,
without pretending to be something that I'm not.
Under the water, I'm free.
Here I can be loud,
I can scream or be silent.
No one else than me watching,
no demands from the world above.
I relax and float, I sink,
I move without moving,
be without thinking.
Exist without acting.
Here I'm free,
free to be me.

65.

I can see you now,
I can see what I'm not.
Why did I hold on so long?
I must have loved you.

66.

The night is dark.
My soul is suffering.
Anxiety is covering me like a wet blanket.
Forgive me. I'm dying slowly,
help me to set my spirit free.
I'm running through the forest like a wild deer,
run, run, till I can run no more.
Exhausted, I lie down on the bare ground.
Too tired to move,
too tired to go any further.
Let it stop here and now.
Let the end of suffering be upon me.
I am no more.
I just am,
I am.

67.

Kneel down beside me,
hold my hand,
I will see your true self,
I will see you beyond your mask,
I will see into your heart,
into the silence of your own vibration.

68.

Woodland, empty space,
meadows, river flowing through,
gently.
Bird sitting in the tree,
watching the world go by.
The world says nothing about the bird.
The world does not see the bird.
Bird sitting peacefully in the tree,
watching the world go by.

69.

In the attic of the mind,
do you live there?
Why are you not awake?
Leave the illusionary comfort of being somebody.
Why bother with the stairs when you have a parachute?
Parachute yourself out of your over-cluttered attic,
so full of stuff from the past,
full of memories,
full of promises about the future.
All this mess and dust will choke you.
Open the window and
inhale the air.
It's fresh.
Your life is not in the attic.
Spread your wings and soar.
Move far away,
far enough to lose the gravity of the mind.
Stay as you are,
stay as I AM.

70.

Visit hours are over,
say goodbye to ego mind,
lay down your sword and live in peace.

71.

Somehow we'll make it.
Hand in hand, we walk through life,
striving to wake up.
When we just give up,
we've done everything,
too tired to continue,
then, everything disappears.
The fog of illusion is clearing up.
Everything is clear.
Suddenly we can see that we have always been awake.
No more striving,
just be.
Somehow we made it.

72.

Let me out,
I'm stuck in here,
imprisoned in my own head.
I know I'm the one that holds the key,
but I have forgotten where I put it.
Where am I?
What am I?
Am I inside trying to get out,
or am I outside trying to get in?
Or am I the inside and the outside?
Of what?
Am I the key,
the key to the unwritten question?
The answer lies dormant inside me,
and so do I.

73.

Love me till this body dies,
I will love you still.
There is no after,
it's here and now,
forever,
always a never-ending now.
I will still love you after this body dies.
Sit down with me and sense that I'm here,
always nowhere else.
Nowhere, somewhere, simultaneously.
This body is not me,
I can leave without dying.
I can die without leaving.
I'm not this body.
It's the cover of a book with all the pages
spread around in the universe for no one to read.

74.

Silent world, silent words.
Nothing is talking, and Nothing is listening.

75.

Who is this insane commentator in my head,
talking to me nonstop?
I'm not interested in what it has to say,
but still, I'm going there again and again,
listening, listening,
till I finally realise what I'm doing.
How did I end up here again?
The voice is like a magnet.
If I can turn the magnet around,
will it repel me from this persistent voice?
Relax and focus on something else
than the chattering mind.
There is so much more than this voice,
this surreal commentator.
Is it even real?
How can the pull of such a mundane activity,
be so attractive?
The chatter is such a small thing
compared to all the empty,
beautiful, silent space,
which is really what I am.
I'm vast, empty, silent space.

76.

Slacklining through life.
Stay happy, stay calm, stay focused, stay balanced.
If I lose my balance, everything comes tumbling down.

77.

Wake me up!
I'm lost in the inferno of this absurd reality.
How did I come to be here?
Oblivion struck me
before I had time to realise what was going on.
I was not prepared.
Can one ever be prepared for life?
Life hits you like a gigantic wave.
You have to learn how to surf the waves
before you can walk.
Walk with me,
I'm too tired,
too lost to walk through this thick existence on my own.
The truth is obscured by the mind,
and its mischievous, devastating tricks.
Let me rest.
Let me be strong enough to ignore its enticing stories.
My mind is like a siren,
singing me to sleep.
I'm sleepwalking yet again,
till I realise I'm not doomed to follow this imposture.
I have been here before,
but this time, I will not drown in the noise of the mind,
of the ego,
believing I'm something that I'm not.

I can feel the truth,
I can feel it pulling me.
Urging me to stop,
stop running,
remember.
You're here.
Wake up.

78.

I can see the light.
I can hear the silence within me speaking to me
from far away.
All I ever want to do is to stay in the silence,
let it wrap its empty nothingness around my body
so that I can ascend this noise, this noisy non-reality.
I go deeper within,
without being afraid of nothing.
Nothing will meet me at the core of my being.
Sleep no more. It's time to wake up,
I can feel the pull towards the silence.
The mind's gravitation is losing its grip on me,
and I feel the urge to go further, deeper into myself.
The gravitation of the silence within
is getting hold of me,
I'm floating downstream without fighting,
without trying to go against the current.
I surrender.
I'm free.

79.

I will tell you my story, before my story is gone.
No mind no story.
What's your story?
I'll tell you mine if you tell me yours.
Mine is non-existing.
No mind, no story.
Stay.
Don't hesitate.
Finally, I have found something perfect.
I have found myself.
I have found I.
You and I are one.
No mind, no story.
No one is here.
Only I.
I am.

80.

Words and sounds,
mixed in a wondrous symphony,
moving around in consciousness,
making small openings for you to see the I.
Grab them,
get intoxicated by the moment,
the glimpses that can lead you to who you truly are,
glorious, wondrous symphony of life.

81.

My only one,
I do everything and nothing to be with you,
my beloved.
This body can't take me there.
My soul cries out in painful longing for you,
my only one.
Not any clever thoughts can take me to you,
only further away from you, my beloved.
Cleverness will make me seem to lose you.
My beloved, wait for me,
I'm going everywhere and nowhere to find you.
Don't let me drift further away from you, my only one.
You embrace me, and you and I become one.
We are one.
I am one with you,
as everything and nothing simultaneously.
In this embrace,
we exist as one,
as we always have,
my everything,
my nothing.
My love.

82.

Silent drumming is waking up my heart.
Where have I been slumbering?
The sun is hitting my face,
I open my eyes and see everything so clearly.
Just be, lie here, do nothing, nothing needs to be done,
I can hear the drumming clearly now,
rhythmic silent drumming.
My true self is calling me home.
Never, never here.
Always here.
The distant sound of singing voices
brings love to my heart,
love that has always been here waiting for me to feel,
waiting for me to hear,
to see,
to wake up.

83.

Do I exist, or am I an illusion?

84.

Be newly born every day of your life.
Die every day of your life,
wake up every second to be bewildered,
excited, curious, in love,
in love with life, with its ups and downs.
Be the conscious watcher
of everything life has to offer you
on this short journey.
Be entangled in the drama of life,
without being entangled.
Watch the sound,
watch the thought about the sound.
Watch the feeling about the thought,
watch the interpretation of the feeling.
Isn't it marvellous,
what just one sound can accomplish?

85.

Lost in the dreamland.
Wandering endlessly without direction,
further and further away from the truth.
It's time to find the way back home.
It's time to wake up!

86.

I'm present. I'm your present.

87.

Caress me.
Keep me in your arms,
I'm going to die.
Hold me tight.
I'm disappearing into nothingness
I'm one with the universe.
No need to miss me.
I am here.
Feel me.
Sense me.
Love me.

88.

I can see you, but can you see me?
Can you see me crying inside while I smile at you?
It's not your fault that I'm invisible to this world.
You can cry, and I will lift you up,
but do you know that I'm crying all the time,
crying for you and for everyone, crying for this world,
so that this world doesn't have to cry alone.

89.

Bells are ringing.
I saw you die in my arms,
die to wake up with me.
Stranger things have happened.

90.

Like an angel.
Confusion from being born into a human body,
lost in this universe to fight for myself.
Why did you abandon me?
Was I told what to expect but just forgot,
or have I been here before?
I can feel more than just this lifetime
pulling me down.
Solemnly I walk this path, again and again,
believing it's all new and fresh,
but I can feel it is not true.
Am I walking this path for the last time?
I can see through the illusion now.
I can finally breathe,
It has not all been in vain.
My struggles have not been in vain,
not necessary,
but not in vain.
Like an angel, I will rise again.

91.

Lost in the chatter of the mind.
Step out of the mind,
step out of your world.
Don't stroll down the path of illusion.
Walk confidently, towards nowhere.
Nowhere to be found,
nowhere to be lost.
You're nowhere.
You're now here!

92.

Complicated world,
complicated words.
The best way to communicate is silence,
but even silence can be misunderstood.
I stand here saying nothing.
Why can't you understand my silence?
I'm standing here screaming my head off,
but no sound is coming out.
I have to accept that no one can hear me.
I'm invisible, I'm soundless.
Within my world,
and only within my world do I exist,
but out here, no one can see me,
no one can hear me.
I'm the only one here,
screaming my head off,
in the most beautiful, silent sound.
Loud am I,
when nothing can be heard.
Silence is my language till everyone learns to hear.
Listen and feel the silence within you,
without you.

93.

Forgotten world, beneath the twilight zone,
peaceful, silent.

94.

Swiftly I pass through the shadows.
I can see.
It's a totally different world.
Why can't I stay here?
Why does the mind keep calling me back?
When I'm in my illusionary world
I hear a voice calling me back home.
My precious world is slowly disappearing,
not so precious anymore,
illusion,
distortion,
pain.
Let me stay in reality a bit longer this time,
let me stay for an eternity.
I make swift visits to my illusionary world,
no need to stay there for long,
no need to stay at all.
I say goodbye,
I will not be far away,
I will still see you, but you can't touch me.
I'm gone, out of reach.
Mind can lure me back no more.
Here is my home,
here is where I'll stay.
Here is I.

95.

I have been carrying this rucksack full of stones
my whole life,
never managed to put it down,
not knowing why or how,
always thinking it's part of me.
It's getting too heavy for me to carry much further,
too heavy to even walk.
I crawl into the fire,
letting the fire consume everything.
When it's over, I see that the only thing
the fire consumed was the rucksack.
Light and free, I walk away,
I'm leaving it all behind. I'm free as a bird.
Yet some walk away from the fire
with their stones still in their arms.

96.

Relax, this is not you. It's not even me.

97.

Next stop, eternal nothingness.
I'm getting off here. Will you come with me?
I turn to you, here we go, here comes nothing.
I throw myself off into nothingness without thinking.
Leave thinking behind and join me.
No thinking, no mind, no story,
nothing, no thing.
I left my luggage behind.
I'm finally free.

98.

Seldom have I seen my thoughts so clearly.
I close my eyes and just let them pass,
they're not my thoughts anyway,
just thoughts.
I open my heart to the silence
and let everything just move on its own,
move without me clinging and grasping.
My feelings are not mine,
they are just feelings, let them pass.
I open my heart to emptiness.
I'm one with everything,
I'm one with nothing,
I'm everything,
I'm nothing,
I am.

99.

Total freedom from yourself.
Embrace freedom.
Total freedom from fear.
Embrace fear.
Listen to the music in your body.
Dance your own dance to your own music,
united with the universe's melody of your heart beating.
Dance,
dance to the music of the universe,
dance.
Your heart beats the music of the universe,
which is my heartbeat,
my music too.

100.

Hope leaves me no rest.
Sorrowful beauty,
caresses me till I can feel no more.
Love is endless,
endless, but nowhere to be found.
Take my hand,
Walk with me.
My hunger for nothing makes me go everywhere
when I should go nowhere,
do nothing,
just lie down on the ground,
melt through the ice and
reunite with the earth, the sky, the stars.
I'm nowhere to be found and nowhere to be lost.
Stay with me.
Lie here with me.
I'm done,
I'm done,
I'm gone.

101.

So silent, the mind.
Didn't I use to know you?
It must have been in another life.

102.

The seeker is running through the forest,
taking in the scenery as she passes every branch,
every straw of grass.
The seeker is seeing the forest,
she is not thinking about the forest.
Her love for the trees is not analytic.
She sees, inhales, she feels the forest as if it was herself.
The seeker is the forest.
The seeker is no more,
left is only I.

103.

Nothing ever happens.
Then suddenly Nothing happened.

104.

Walk with me,
don't linger,
being wrapped up in all that is happening,
you are not a happening.
Walk with me, hold my hand,
no need to go anywhere,
stay as the one you are.
Separate yourself from yourself,
and you can stay with me forever.
Don't get distracted.
Without your illusionary made-up version of a self,
you are whole, you're perfect.
Move away from the ego,
and you'll realise that you are more,
not less, without it.
Without your illusion hijacking reality,
you'll see that
You are the eternal Truth,
you're everything and nothing,
you're love, you're beauty.
You Are Everything.

105.

Wake up to life.
It's not what you think it is.
See it. Look and see without your eyes.
Don't think about it. It's not in your mind,
it's all around you,
everything, including you,
without you.

106.

You have been looking for me for so many years.
Stop looking out there,
I'm right here, and so are you.

107.

How to lead when I have fallen?
Fumbling in the dark, I am.
Show me the way, and I will follow.
Show me the way, and I will lead.

108.

I step back from me and touch the ground,
to see if I'm still alive.

109.

The light within is lightening up everything.
Now I can see it,
has it always been here,
obscured by the veil of the mind?

110.

Love poem to my soul.
I lie down before you.
Strip me naked of what I'm not.
I am the truth, the one and only truth.
I am nothing.
I AM.
I'm the beginning and the end.
There is only one.
There is only I.
I AM is nothing.
I AM.

111.

In my silence, I say to you how much I love you,
more than any words can ever say.
In my silence, I can feel how much I love you,
more than I can possibly express in words.
I love you!

In memory of my brother